Becoming Me

A programmed autobiography

Format developed by Dr. Linda C. Beattie Inlow

© 1998 by Linda C Beattie Inlow

First Printing September 1998
Published and distributed in the United States by:
Kopacetic inK, PO Box 323, Kalama, WA 98625
(360) 673-1743 (fax) or email books@kalama.com

Edited by: Kathryn Doll
Printing: Gorham Printing

ISBN 0-9619634-3-3

Kopacetic inK

Printed in the United States of America

This book is dedicated to all those who have helped me to be the person I am, as well as to those in the future who continue to support my journey of *becoming me*.

Note to the Author

This book is for you. It is about you. In it you may tell what you feel and think about yourself, your family, the neighborhood, school and the world.

It is important you answer honestly. Say what you think. Write down what you feel. Draw what you see. Nothing you do will be wrong, for you are the author. This book is all about and for you.

If someone else were writing about you, he would ask all sorts of questions to find out who you were, where and when you were born, what kind of family you have, even what your favorite things are. The same is true in your book, <u>BECOMING ME</u>. You share how you came to be, where you are, and where you think you and your world are going.

Instead of someone asking you the questions, you will simply complete the sentence or thought in your own words or art. There are even blank pages for you to write your own personal thoughts, hopes, dreams or reflections.

It's tough business writing a book, especially a book about your personal life story. I hope you enjoy the discovery of the special person you are becoming[1].

LCBI

PS You don't have to start at page one!!

---

[1] No matter what age, we are all in a state of becoming. Psychologists call it maturation. Human beings never cease learning and growing until life is over.

Note to Parents

Dear Parent,

These pages belong to your child alone. Herein the child is encouraged to complete phrases in a word, by complete thoughts or through art. All ideas, comments, and actions should be from your child and not merely reflections of what you feel is proper and correct.

Since you are looking at this book, you must be a caring parent. You care how your child is developing. You want your child to be healthy emotionally as well as psychically. Give your child the freedom to respond out of his or her own unique creative self.

Some of the most brilliant and talented individuals the world has produced like Albert Einstein, Vincent van Gogh, and Ben Franklin, were thwarted by well intentioned people who made comments such as, "That will never work,", "That's absurd," or "You can't say/do that." Your child may or may not be as talented or brilliant an individual as those mentioned above; certainly your child is *unique*.

Allow him or her the freedom to express this uniqueness. Let your child discover his or her foundations in self-esteem, self-identity, and begin to experience some self-confidence with the help of these pages. Should the child need assistance in the reading or writing of the text, give aid, but nothing more.

Thank-you for caring enough to let your child discover the becoming self.

Sincerely,

Dr. Linda C. Beattie Inlow

Table of Contents

SELF

Vital Statistics	p. 1
Firsts in My Life	p. 3
Self-Portrait	p. 7
My Favorite Things	p. 12
Hand-Print	p. 17
Future Predictions	p. 21
General Information	p. 22

FAMILY

Family Tree	p. 27
Home	p. 28
Pets	p. 39
Beliefs	p. 43
Place of Worship	p. 48

SCHOOLS

Schools Attended	p. 54
Sports	p. 57
Lessons	p. 57
"IF"	p. 60
Using My Imagination	p. 63
Artist's Concept	p. 67
My Opinion	p. 71
"IF" continued...	p. 72

NEIGHBORHOOD

Neighborhood Places	p. 77
Roles People Play	p. 92
Map of Neighborhood	p. 99
Friends and Neighbors	p. 101
Colors	p. 106

WORLD

"IF ..."	p. 109
Least Favorite Things	p. 112
What in the World	p. 114
World Problems	p. 117
World Vision	p. 119
Environment	p. 120
The World That Is To Come	p. 123

Answers to Riddles   p. 126

Becoming Me

_____
(name)

Life Story (so far)

SELF

Vital Statistics

Name:

Current Address:

My life began at   a.m./p.m. on   (month)

       (date)   (year) at

       (place) in   (city).

On the day I was born the weather was

The following people were in attendance:

At the time I was born the following people were my family:

At birth I weighed

I was   inches long. My hair color was

My eyes are

I cut my first tooth at (age)

My nationality/heritage includes

My name came from

My name may have another meaning. For example, David means *blessed* in Hebrew, Linda means *pretty* in Spanish, Charles means *manly* in Old English. **My name means**

This is a picture of me at age

PHOTO

Currently I am _____ feet _____ inches tall.

    I weigh

    My eyes are

Firsts in My Life

I lost my first tooth at   (age). It happened when

The earliest thing I can remember is

I walked for the first time

The first word I spoke was

The first word I read was

My best friend's name is

The first time I rode a tricycle I

The first time I rode a bike

The first time I took the train was

The first time ever in a boat I

On my first airplane ride I

Some of the first things I did to help someone were

I remember my first day at school. I

The first birthday party I remember, I

My first really best friend was

MORE STORIES ABOUT MY EARLY YEARS

Self-Portrait

Personal Reflections

At my last birthday

For my next birthday

Joy means

I would go to _____ if I had a problem.
     (name of person)

Some things that really bug me

The biggest problem I've had so far

What I like most about myself is

What others like about me

My friend thinks I'm

My parent(s) think I'm

The funniest thing I've ever done

What I dislike about myself is

Something that really bugs my parents is when I

I'm a pretty special kid. I can do some things very well and some things not so well. One thing I do best is

Using my imagination is fun. Sometimes I imagine

Sometimes I daydream about

My happiest dream was

The strangest dream I ever had was

When I was little dreams could sometimes be scary. Once I was afraid of

It's okay to be fearful. Even today, I sometimes fear

Love means

On the weekends I usually

During the week my schedule includes

On a typical Wednesday I

Sometimes I watch TV. Some of the programs I enjoy are

When I'm not watching TV, I

My Favorite Things

Some of my favorite things are

My favorite relative is

My best friend is

My favorite color is

My favorite food is

My favorite sport is

My favorite clothes are

My favorite music is

My favorite vegetable is

My favorite ice cream is

                     is my favorite drink.

                                                          is my favorite toy.

                                                          is my favorite animal.

                                                          is my favorite number.

                                                          is my favorite cartoon character.

                                                          is my favorite movie.

                                                          is my favorite computer game.

The best pizza is

The best holiday is

My best birthday was

The best television program ever was/is

My favorite TV show is

The best board game to play is

The best computer game to play is

The best game to play is

The best movie I've ever seen was

_____ is my favorite video.

_____ is my favorite song.

_____ is my favorite season.

_____ is my favorite animal.

_____ is my favorite story.

_____ is my favorite singing group.

My favorite poem is

My favorite person in history is _____ because

My favorite person is _____ because

My favorite place to eat is

My favorite candy is

My favorite music group is

My favorite car is _____ because

My favorite TV star is

My favorite book is _____ because

My favorite storybook character is _____
because

My favorite place to go is

My favorite actor is

My favorite outfit to wear is

                                                                         is my favorite day of the week.

                                                                          is my favorite all time dessert.

                                                                          is my favorite CD because

                                                                          is my favorite tape.

is/was my favorite friend at bedtime.

Other favorite things include:

Hand Print

Age _____ Date _____

Personal Reflections

Drawing/Photo of Me and My Family

Personal Reflections

Future Predictions

By the time I'm thirty (30) I'll

In the future I will be _____ feet _____ inches in

height and weigh _____.

By the time I'm thirty-five (35) I will

wear glasses	Yes	No
have braces	Yes	No
be bald	Yes	No
have a car	Yes	No
graduate from high school	Yes	No
go to college	Yes	No
buy a home	Yes	No
live in an apartment	Yes	No
live on a farm	Yes	No
get married	Yes	No
have children	Yes	No
have pets	Yes	No
have at least one career	Yes	No

and:

When I grow up I will own

When I grow up I will play with

When I'm older I want to live

General Information

Things that make me laugh

The funniest joke I know

What really scares me is

If I could make something disappear, I'd

Once I broke

The adult I admire most is _____ because

When I am alone I

If I could choose another name to call myself it would be _____
because

My nickname is

I get mad when

If I met someone for the first time and had to tell them about myself I would say,

If I described myself to someone who could not see I would say:

If I had to choose a special friend, it would be _____

because

On Saturdays I

For snacks I enjoy

On a hot summer afternoon I like to drink

I am the _____ (number) child in my family. I have _____(number) brothers/sisters. The name(s) of my family members:

Me having fun.

Personal Reflections

FAMILY

Family Tree

_____	_____	_____	_____
Great Grandfather	Great Grandfather	Great Grandfather	Great Grandfather
+	+	+	+
_____	_____	_____	_____
Great Grandmother	Great Grandmother	Great Grandmother	Great Grandmother
|	|	|	|

_____ _____   _____ _____
Paternal Grandfather & Grandmother   Maternal Grandfather & Grandmother
                \   /

_____   _____
    Father   Mother
           married on _____
           married at _____
Aunts/Uncles: :Aunts/Uncles
                    \   /

                    _____
                              ME

Brothers/Sisters:

HOME

A house is

A home is

The difference between a house and home

Currently these people live in my home:

My favorite room

When I think of home I think

My first memory about my house is

If I were to design the perfect house it would include:

swimming pool	country kitchen
Jacuzzi	hot tub
bedrooms	sauna
game room	computer room
be in the city	be in the country
be in suburbs	____# of bathrooms

be one level	be _____ levels
have a fireplace	have a woodstove
special library	worship center
garage	playroom
own bedroom	fenced yard
and?????	

To make my current home better I would

Currently my bedroom

The best bedroom I've every seen had

The perfect bedroom would look like

Around the house I

Some of my chores are

If I were a parent I would

The best mom would

The best dad would

My favorite mom besides my own is _____ because

My favorite dad besides my own is _____ because

To be a parent means

I would like to help my parent(s)

_____ is something I really look forward to doing around the house whenever I want.

A happy home includes:

and/or	honesty	trust	forgiveness
	respect	freedom	communication
	shared fun	love	privacy
	hugs	kisses	"I love you"
	religion	God	smiles

My Family

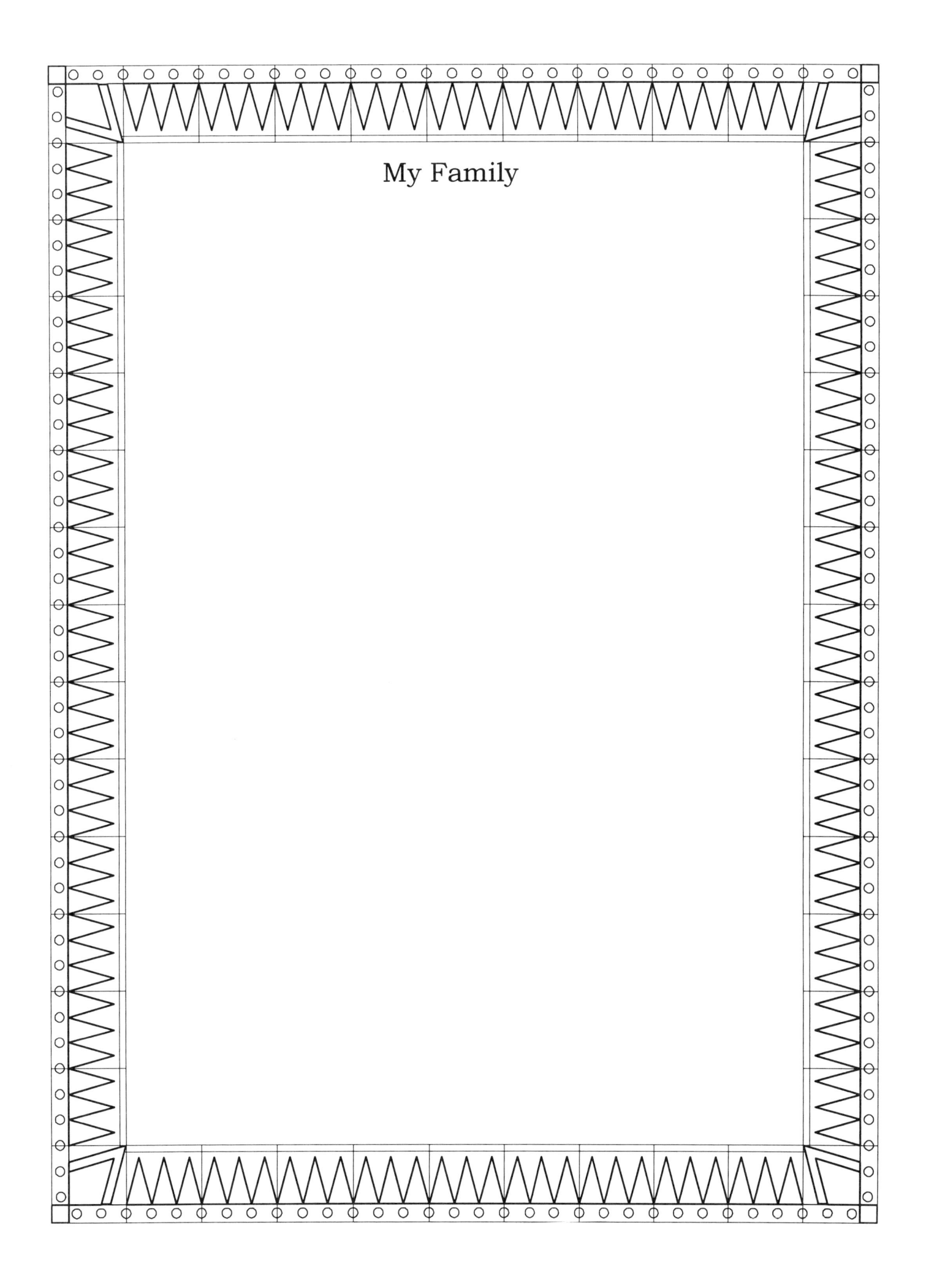

Personal Reflections

My Home

Personal Reflections

To make my home better I

Some of the things I like to do for others

I really like it when my parent

If I had free use of the telephone I'd call

If I cooked dinner we'd eat

If I had a party I would invite

If I didn't have my parents and I could choose anybody in the world I would choose _____ for my mother and

_____ for my father.

Parents really shouldn't

The people who make up my family include

When the whole family gets together we

If someone in my family were hurt

The most famous person in our family

The best family vacation we

Some of the places my family likes to go

Some of the places we vacation

The best vacation for me

Holidays are, for many, family times. At _____
(Thanksgiving/Fourth of July, etc.) my family

On _____ (special holiday i.e. Christmas/Hanukkah) we

The best holiday time I remember

My family during a special holiday.

Personal Reflections

Marriage means

When I become a parent

To make a happy family

The key to a happy family life

Some at home family projects I have enjoyed

PETS

The pets my family has had include

(List)　　　　NAME　　　　　　　　　　TYPE OF ANIMAL

My special pet

My favorite animal for a pet

If I could have *any* animal for a pet

The most unusual pet

If I were an animal I'd be					because

The animal who is most like me

My Pet(s)

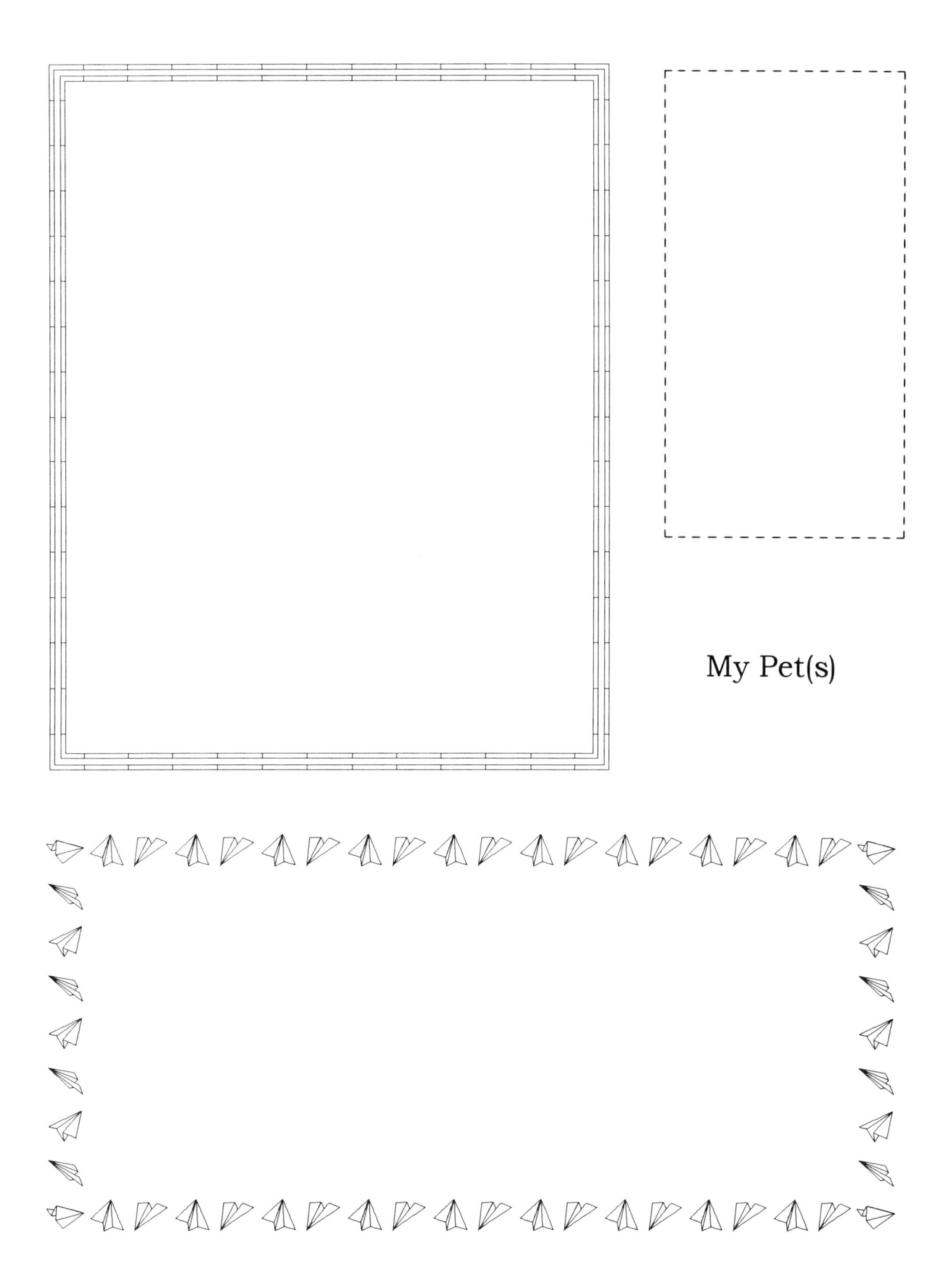

Personal Reflections

BELIEFS

Who a person is, is often reflected in his or her family's religious or spiritual beliefs. These could center around a Supreme Being known as God, Jesus, Confucius, Buddha, a positive energy force or a set of guidelines or rules which govern the way a person should live or act towards others. Respond to the following according to your traditions or beliefs. If a phrase or word is inappropriate i.e. God should be Jehovah or Yahweh, then cross it out and write the appropriate word.

Historically my family has gone to services at

Today my family worships at

The best place to think about God is

I know their is a positive force in my life when

Personally, when I think of a Supreme Being, I imagine

My family considers worship

To behave with kindness toward another means

Sometimes when I think about the bad in the world, I wonder

When something bad happens, I

Evil exists because

Sometimes I get mad at _____ for letting negative things occur.

Sometimes I wonder why certain things are as they are like

To be mad at God

In my house God

When we worship we go to

Prayer means

I believe in God means

Jesus is

In my family we use these words to talk about faith

God wants me

God loves me

God knows

If God and I were to meet face to face

I want to ask God

I want to know why

I call God

God and I talk when

I feel closest to God when

To have faith, a person

To have faith in God means

To have faith in myself means

To talk to God I

My favorite prayer is

Death means

When someone dies,

If I know someone who dies, I

"To love the Lord" means

The best place to be with God is

To describe how I feel about God I

If I met someone who didn't know about God, I would tell them

When I meet someone who doesn't believe or think the way I do, I

Some of the belief systems/religions I want to learn about

PLACE OF WORSHIP

There are many different ways and places to worship i.e. synagogue, temple, church, etc. There are different names for the people who assist in that worship i.e., pastor, priest, rabbi, brother, minister. There are different Holy Words i.e. Talmud, Koran, Old Testament, New Testament, Bible used in our place of worship. There are different names for places to educate young people about their faith. For convenience the words church, pastor, Bible, Sunday School, *and* Vacation Bible School *have been used in the following statements. Should these words not reflect your lifestyle or place of worship, please substitute the correct one. Thank you.*

The place I worship is

One of my favorite places to talk to God is

Sermons should

If I preached I would tell people

Church is people. People should

If I could change anything about my place of worship

I like the following things in at my place of worship:

guitar playing	sermons	prayers
singing	choir	children's sermons
kneeling	giving money	reading Scripture
silence	windows	praising God
organ music	my pastor	the people
my friends	Sunday School	peace

AND

My favorite story in the Bible

My favorite verse in the Bible

I like   (name) in the Bible because

My favorite story in the Old Testament is

The story I like best about God

A Christian

A Jew

A Buddhist

A believer

Praise means

My favorite religious holiday is

When my favorite religious holiday comes, I

To help me remember Holy Days I

Sunday School

Vacation Church School

My church helps others by

If I could volunteer and help I would

What makes my place of worship unique is

One of my most special times at my place of worship was

My special place to talk to God

Personal Reflections

SCHOOL

Most of my life has been spent learning.   When I was a baby I first learned to

and

and

and   .

When I was a toddler, about 18 months to three years old I learned

to

and

and

and   .

I have learned a lot from just observing other people. I have learned to

Now that I am more fully-grown I continue to learn from others. Some of the things I am learning to do are

Now that I am older I go to school. I started attending school when I was

These are the schools I have attended include:

SCHOOL	GRADE	YEAR	TEACHER

As a student I am

TRUE/FALSE

____ I am a curious person

____ I am very industrious.

____ I am an ambitious person.

____ I am energetic.

____ One could call me shy.

____ I ask a lot of questions.

____ I kind of do things at the last minute.

____ I am an intelligent human being.

____ I am a caring person.

____ One could say I am a bright student.

____ Sometimes I am slow to catch on to things.

____ I enjoy reading.

____ Math is my favorite subject.

____ Math is just something I need to learn.

____ Computer science is always a challenge.

____ I enjoy spending time on the computer.

____ Learning a foreign language could be fun.

____ I like learning about other people.

____ History can be boring.

TRUE/FALSE cont.

    ____ I find history exciting.

    ____ Music is a wonderful thing to study.

    ____ I look forward to learning an instrument.

    ____ I enjoy singing songs.

    ____ Recess is my favorite time of day.

    ____ One could say I am artistic.

    ____ I enjoy art.

    ____ I think art and art projects should be done by somebody else!

    ____ Telling stories or writing them is fun.

    ____ Reading is important to me.

    ____ Knowing about my country is important.

The most important things in the true/false are:

Things in the true/false list I might want to change are:

My best art project was

The biggest surprise was

My favorite teacher so far has been   because

My favorite subject in pre-school was

My favorite time at elementary school was

At middle school I enjoy

The best thing about school

My school colors are

Someday I would like to attend

I like books about

I really am good at

During the week my favorite time of day is

I wish my teacher(s) knew

The best day of the week at school is because

SPORTS

So far I have participated in: (circle all that are appropriate)

volleyball	ballet	soccer	T-ball
tennis	football	ice hockey	roller-skating
rollerblading	swimming	water polo	skateboarding
martial arts	rugby	field hockey	weight lifting
baseball	softball	diving	Little League

and:

I really enjoy watching sports. I've seen the following sports in action:

A sports figure I admire is   because

LESSONS

Being a child means

When I was a little kid I thought someone my age was

In school I like to

I love studying about

Something I find really difficult is

I can hardly wait to learn more about (circle all that apply)

    computers   the stars   storybooks   agriculture

    foreign language   animals   my body   politics

    numbers/math   plants   recycling   earth

and:

Do You Know these riddles?[1]

Who speaks every language?

What did the man get when he stole the calendar?

In what month people talk least?

Why the little inkspots cried?

What a spendthrift saves and a miser spends?

What makes the Tower of Pisa lean?

What is broken every time you say its name?

Why couldn't Eve get the measles?

My favorite riddle:

My favorite joke

Life's biggest lesson so far has been

In the next four years I would like to know

---

[1] The answers to these riddles are on page 136

I am currently taking lessons in:

I have been or would like to be active in or learn more about:
(circle all that apply)

karate	taekwon-do	swimming	computers
tap	ballet	exercise	singing
golf	archery	scuba	snorkeling
tennis	volleyball	soccer	guitar
band	orchestra	music	pep rally
kung fu	spinning	ballroom dance	tai chi
painting	watercolor	foreign language	cooking

and:

Fill in the blanks with words beginning with the first letter in the line:

	BODY PART	CITY	FLOWER	FOOD
S				
T				
U				
D				
E				
N				
T				

If I could change anything about school

I think we should study

My ideal junior high/middle school schedule would include:

PE	computer	biology	Home Ec.
Woodshop	Art	science	metal shop
choir	foreign language	reading	writing
theater	orchestra	poetry	history
wellness	health	outdoor education	math

and:

IF.....

If I found $5.00 in a parking lot, I would

If I found money in a store, I would

If a friend took something from a store, I would

If I saw a bully hurting a little kid, I would

If a stranger came up to me and offered me a ride, I would

If I saw someone drop a wallet by accident, I would

If I lost something important to me and a friend found it, I would

If a friend offered me pills to make me "feel good" I would

If I saw another student with something dangerous I would

If I were to invent the greatest toy, it would look like this:

This is what it does:

This is how it works:

Personal Reflections

If I could play a musical instrument,

My parents would like to learn

Growing old means

I really feel proud when

USING MY IMAGINATION

If I could, after school I would

When the sun is out and school is on, I

When its raining I like to

The wind

Snow makes me

Breezes on a sunny afternoon make me

Given these three items I could make

material	thread	needle	=
plastic	hose	sprinkler	=
paper	sticks	string	=
dirt	water	spoon	=
tree	rope	wood	=
flour	salt	water	=
tire	stick	rope	=
tire rim	box	plastic	=
box	material	tape	=
paper	scissors	tape	=
newspaper	scissors	glue	=

Of all the books I've ever read I've enjoyed _____
In the story....

My favorite storybook character is

Of all the characters I've read about I think _____
is most like me, because

Of all the characters I've read about I would like for one day to be

From all the movies I've seen, I'd like to act in

The movie star I'd like to talk to is

We'd talk about

I'd ask

The person in history I would like to meet is

I would ask

Of all the people I know, I think I look most like

PERSONAL REFLECTIONS

ARTIST'S CONCEPT

I can make great faces. Here is a picture of me smiling.

This is a picture of me frowning.

PERSONAL REFLECTIONS

ARTIST'S CONCEPT

This is a face full of surprise

Photo or Drawing

Photo or Drawing

This is my mad face.

PERSONAL REFLECTIONS

IN MY OPINION

In my opinion a police officer

A minister must

A computer

My favorite thing about babies

The best thing about older people

My favorite thing about my classmate

Freedom is

Brotherhood/Sisterhood mean

I fear

The best thing about getting older is

....has a mean sound.

....sounds soft.

....is the most sensitive person I know.

....is the most beautiful person.

If I were to put something very special to me in a time vault and open it in thirty years, my friends and family would find the following items:

"IF"

If I wrote a book, it would be about

If I could be any animal,

If I were a bird, I'd be

If I were a fish, I'd be

If I could live anywhere, it would be

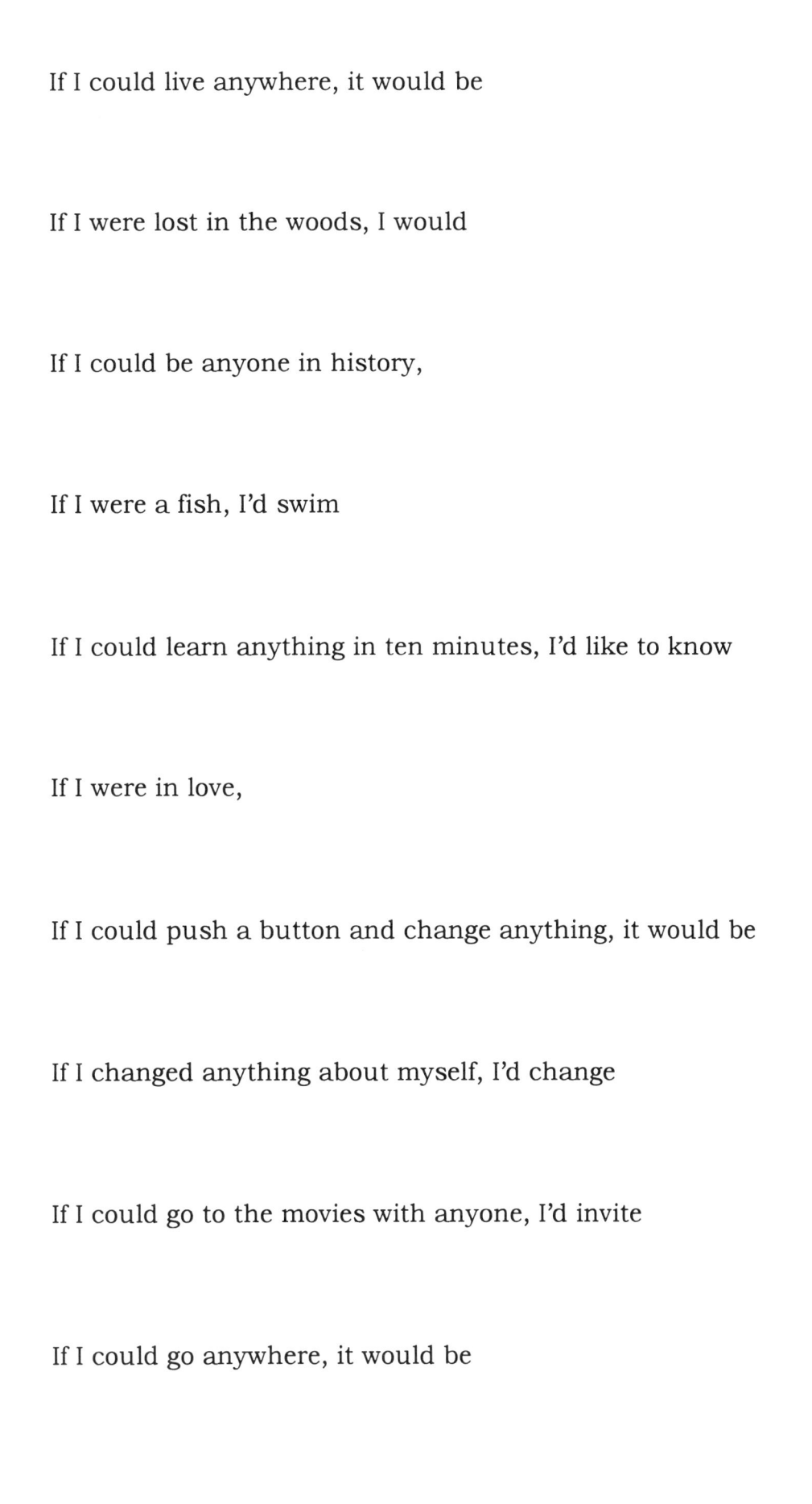

If I were lost in the woods, I would

If I could be anyone in history,

If I were a fish, I'd swim

If I could learn anything in ten minutes, I'd like to know

If I were in love,

If I could push a button and change anything, it would be

If I changed anything about myself, I'd change

If I could go to the movies with anyone, I'd invite

If I could go anywhere, it would be

PERSONAL REFLECTIONS

Using only a square, circle and triangle - draw a school

PERSONAL REFLECTIONS

NEIGHBORHOOD

NEIGHBORHOOD PLACES

In my neighborhood one would see

Next door lives

On the other side lives

Across the road is

The nearest grocery store is

The best video store

My favorite place to play in the neighborhood

My place of worship is just

In my neighborhood the school

The kinds of trees around my home are

The kinds of flowers one would see in my neighborhood are

        roses   daffodils   tulips

        daises   gladiolas   lilies

        pansies   petunias   dahlias

and

My favorite flower to look at

My favorite colors for flowers are

My favorite flower to smell

_____ grows the best garden in the neighborhood.

The best house to play at

When in a dark place like my closet or attic I imagine

Attics are great places to

Garages and basements

In my home there are rooms. Here is a small map of the inside of my house.

FLOOR PLAN OF MY HOME

PERSONAL REFLECTIONS

The kind of trees one sees in my neighborhood are

Douglas fir	apple	hawthorn	cedar
hemlock	pear	apricots	plum
dogwood	willow	oak	peach
Chinese plum	weeping willow	spruce	birch
cherry	apricot	pine	nectarine

and:

LIBRARY

At the library I

The best books to read are under

The best book I've ever read

The best book ever read to me

My favorite author/series

If I wrote another book it would be about

Magazines I read

Reading

COMPUTERS

If I were to design a computer,

If I created a computer game, it would

The best thing about computers

My favorite computer game

My favorite computer program

I use the computer

CAMP

If I went camping, I would take

Going to camp

If I go camping, I would go

The most fun camping was

The best practical joke played at camp

The funniest camp song I know

While camping I enjoy   getting firewood   hiking
        swimming   exploring   investigating caves
        fishing   roasting marshmallows   the fire
        making s'mores   cook outs   hunting
        getting dirty   going barefoot   sleeping outside
        telling scary stories   sleeping in a tent
        seeing stars   clean air   wading in creeks
and...

PICNIC
On a picnic

I wear

Four people I would invite on a picnic:

We would eat

We would take

We would play

ZOO

At the zoo

At the zoo I enjoy

The animals

There is never enough time to watch

The funniest animal

The most unusual animal

If I could be any animal, it would be because

If I were to work at the zoo, I'd like to

FAIR
At the fair

At the midway where all the games arc I

Exhibits at the fair

When I go to the county fair, I like

The best rides are

At the fair I enjoy eating

cotton candy	hot dogs	Italian ice	hamburgers
elephant ears	popcorn	nuts	corn on the cob
pizza	tacos	churros	funnel cakes

DEPARTMENT STORE/THE MALL

My favorite place to shop in my hometown is

My favorite kind of store to shop in

If I could go to the mall with my friend, I'd choose

When shopping I like to

My favorite kind of movie to watch is

I would go see _____(actor) in any movie.

I also like (actors)

The movie I've seen the most is

My family has these videos

The most popular ones are

I wish we owned

If I were to write and direct a **movie,** the character's names would be:

I'd have them....

The story would...

PERSONAL REFLECTIONS

GROCERY STORE

At the market I want to buy

My folks like to buy

My favorite food to snack on is

My favorite meal is

I really like to eat

When I'm thirsty I like to drink

If I have to, I'll drink

I really should eat more

The cupboard's bare. Someone gave me $25.00 to buy groceries. My list of purchases would include:

When it comes to fast food I like to go to

If someone mentions "junk food," I think of

My favorite snack foods are *(circle)*

    pizza   M & M's   ice cream   Snickers   peanuts

    popcorn   cotton candy   pie   licorice   cake

    Twinkies   potato chips   chips   cookies   pretzels

and:

PARK

My favorite park to play at

The best thing to do at a park is *(circle)*

    talk with friends   roll in the grass   ride bike

    use playground   use my imagination   swing

    rollerblade   slide   play ball

    read a book   picnic   play frisbee

    and

My town's park has

NEIGHBORHOOD NEEDS

A young boy in the South saw a hungry man in the street. He went home and convinced his parents to let him share a pillow, blanket and hot cup of coffee with the stranger. His charitable act caught the attention of others. Now a feeding and housing program exists in his neighborhood for street people.

In my neighborhood I think we need

If I had the power and authority to make my neighborhood a better place to live, I would

If I were mayor of my city, I would make the following promises to the people

Most of my friends are concerned about

The biggest problem we face today is

What bothers me most

The environment is an issue

People should be more concerned with

ROLES PEOPLE PLAY

A person must be many things in life. Right now, I am

The following are definitions I give to the roles people play:

    Child:

    Learner:

    Companion:

Household Worker:

Money Manager:

Breadwinner:

Parent:

Disciplinarian:

Teacher:

Friend:

Brother/Sister:

Grandparent:

Worker:

Student:

Believer:

Sinner:

Saint:

Best Friend:

ENERGY

The best source of energy comes from

In my house our energy comes from

In my town we can use the following kinds of energy in our homes and places of business:

    nuclear power   the sun   geo-thermic   oil

    hydro-electric   natural gas wind   coal

When I think about using nuclear energy,

Solar energy in the future

If I were to design an energy efficient home, it would

Some special features of my home would include: *(circle)* sauna

    swimming pool hot tub   acres of land   fireplace

    tennis court   pool room movie room   computer room

    and:

My furniture would look like

My plants would

RESOURCES

The most valuable resource today

Water in the year 2100 will be

The water in my area is

As a natural resource oil

Natural gas in my area

In the year 2050 I imagine air will be

Coal by the year 2050

The air in my town

To improve the quality of our water we should

To improve the quality of air the citizens can

TRANSPORTATION

In the past five years I have used the following means of transportation: *(circle)*

| stroller | carseat | booster | city bus | car | skateboard |

skates　　rollerblades　feet　　pogo stick　moped　BART

tricycle　　bike　　　3-wheeler　helicopter　horse　subway

infant backpack　　　ice skates　jet　　　airplane

llama　　donkey　　ostrich　　train　　school bus

and:

Someday I want to drive

Our family drives

Automobiles in the future will

The main source of public transportation in the future will be:

PERSONAL REFLECTIONS

A MAP OF MY NEIGHBORHOOD

Draw a map of the neighborhood. Include the most important places, where you play, live, friend's live, worship, shop, etc...

N
W + E
S

PERSONAL REFLECTIONS

FRIENDS AND NEIGHBORS

The most important person in my life is

My best friend in the neighborhood and I

Before I started school my best friend was

As a friend, God would like me to

God can be my friend. God fits into my life

A good neighbor does

If I had to move from this neighborhood and could only take three things, I would take:

     1.

     2.

     3.

I feel very sad when

My best friend and I talk about

To earn money I

Girls are

Boys are

My best girl friend and I

My best boy friend and I

I really enjoy people who

My favorite games to play around the house are

My friends think I am *(circle)*

witty   pretty   handsome   charming   shy   reserved
smart   healthy   practical   fun   talkative   intuitive
quiet   good sport   average   moody   clown   clumsy
and:

My best friend and me.

PERSONAL REFLECTIONS

The worst part about growing up is

The best part about getting older is

My best advice to those younger than I would be

I think the ideal age to be is   , because

To be an adult means

A president should always

If I could vote

Imagine owning a neighborhood store. Inside it would have

If I could give anything to the poor it would be

Currently my neighbors and I

To be neighborly means

COLORS IN MY LIFE

A rainbow reminds me of

When I see the color yellow, I feel

The color of spring would naturally be

Summer is the time to

Summer is the color of

The favorite thing I like about fall

Fall colors include

In winter I love

The color I choose for winter is

Every color can mean something. Some think blue is cool or reminds one of a warm bright summer sky. The following colors remind me of something and make me feel:

COLOR	MEMORY	FEELING
red		
purple		
green		
orange		
yellow		
gold		
violet		
black		
brown		
white		
blue		
silver		
gray		

My favorite colors to wear are: red   green   dusty rose
   purple   violet   black   gray   yellow
   white   pink   lime   brown   orange

   light blue   navy   blue   tan   khaki

and:

If I were to be a color it would be _____
because

The colors of the following emotions are

    Love -

    Joy -

    Disappointment -

    Happiness

    Sorrow

    Laughter

    Anger

    Envy

    Jealousy

    Sadness

    Pride

    Surprise

    Awe

WORLD

IF.....

If I could travel anywhere n the world right this minute, I would go

While there I would

If I could travel the world and take three people, I would take:

We would go to _____

and then hop a plane for _____.

Someday I would like to go to *(circle)*

		China	Japan	Korea
Germany	Mongolia	India	Thailand	Kenya
Africa	South Africa	Sudan	Israel	Egypt
Turkey	Russia	Greece	Italy	France
Spain	Mexico	Argentina	Antarctica	Canada
North Pole	England	Scotland	Ireland	Peru
Columbia	Panama	Australia	Timbuktu	Tahiti

and:

I have already visited

The States I have visited in America, include

If I were President of the United States of America these would be my opinions about what we should do in world affairs:

   the poor:

   war:

   weapons:

   education:

   prisons:

   lawbreakers:

   guns:

   housing:

food:

health care:

the elderly:

peace:

space:

freedom:

human rights:

I think grownups should settle differences by

War is

The worst thing about war

If I could be numbered among the travelers into space, I would want to go to

I would expect to find

If I could go to Space Camp, I'd want to learn all about

If I had lots of money, I would

If I had helped God create the world, I would have

If I could cure a disease, it would be _____ because

LEAST FAVORITE THINGS

My least favorite color

My least favorite food

My least favorite sport

My least favorite clothing

My least favorite teacher

My least favorite music

My least favorite vegetable

My least favorite person

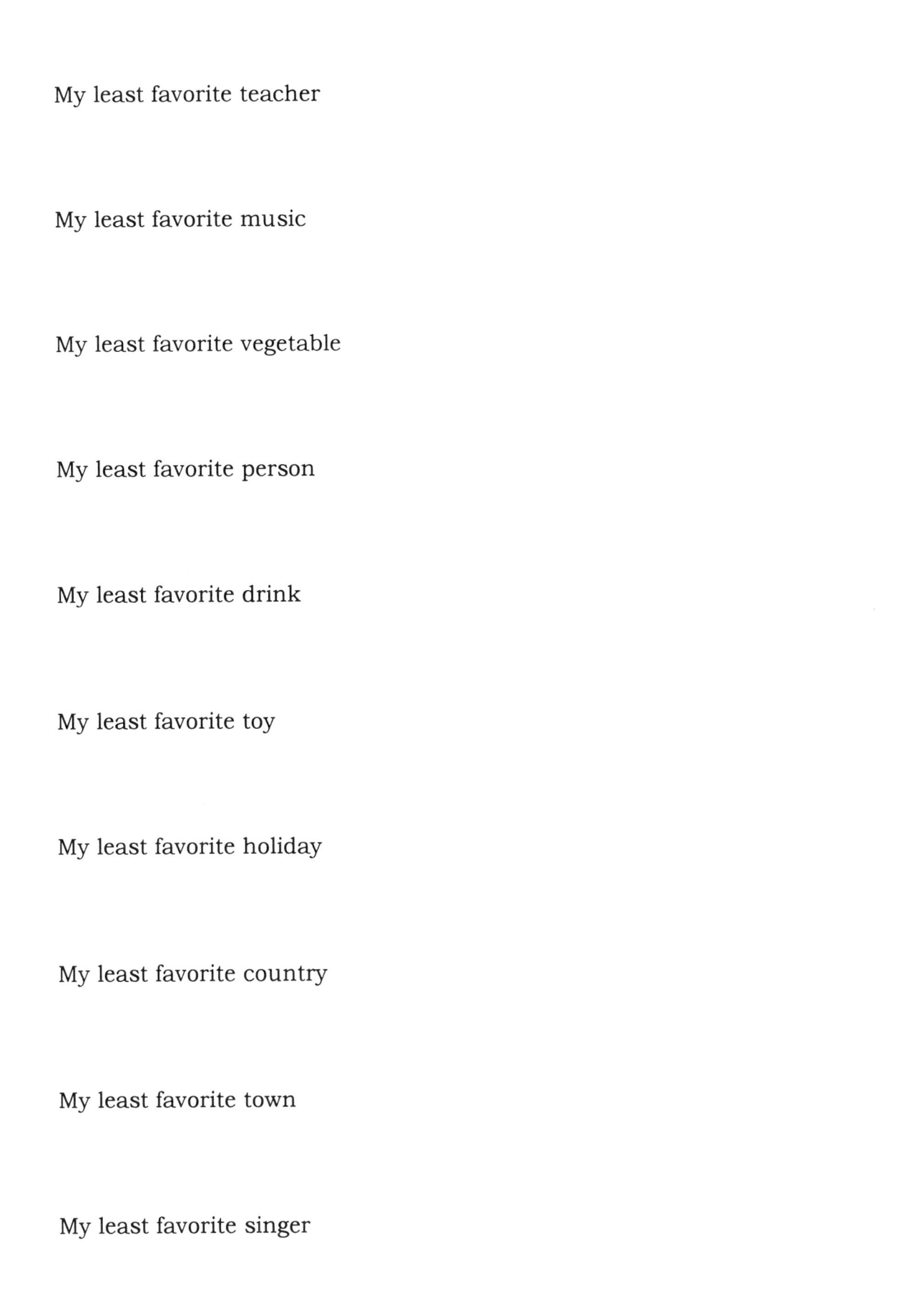

My least favorite drink

My least favorite toy

My least favorite holiday

My least favorite country

My least favorite town

My least favorite singer

My least favorite way to spend time is

The thing I'd like to change about me is

And my least favorite thing is

WHAT IN THE WORLD

Fill in the blanks with things that begin with the first letters of *earth*.

MINERAL	ANIMAL	FOOD	NATION	RIVER
E	E	E	E	E
A	A	A	A	A
R	R	R	R	R
T	T	T	T	T
H	H	H	H	H

MY WORLD

PERSONAL REFLECTIONS

WORLD PROBLEMS

There are many problems in the world. If I were a world leader, I would solve the following problems by.....

World Hunger -

No Money -

Boundary Disputes -

Religious Differences -

Racial Tension -

Large Debts -

Water Pollution -

Air Pollution -

Oil Shortage -

Oil Monopolies -

AIDS -

Cancer -

Radiation Leakage -

Terrorism -

Race to Space -

Chemical Pollution -

Lack of Communication -

UFO's -

Solving the world's problems continued,
Military -

Over population -

Depletion of the ozone layer -

Violence in the schools -

Gangs -

WORLD VISION

To make this world a better place we must

It order to make it happen I would

Some other things I would change are

Environment: What Can Be Done?

In order to make the environment cleaner and the world a healthier place to live my family and I *(check all that apply/ circle what the family might do)*

RECYCLE: __ newspapers __ oil __ magazines __ milk jugs

__ tin cans __ aluminum cans __ mixed paper __ cardboard

__ plastic __ green glass __ clear glass __ all glass

and:

SHARE: __ clothing with others __ shoes __ food __ labor

__ books __ talents __ time __ a hug

and:

HEALTH: __ eat low fat foods __ eat non-processed foods

__ exercise __ reduce sugar intake __ brush teeth

__ no smoking __ say no to drugs __ vaccinations

__ wear seatbelts __ low fat diets __ cut down on red meats

__ yearly check ups __ see a dentist and:

AIR POLLUTION: ___ use alternative transportation

I..... ___ walk as much as possible.

    ___ use a bicycle, skateboard or scooter instead of a vehicle

    ___ car pool with friends.

    ___ write letters to companies that affect my air, water and home asking for their help

    ___ ride the bus

    ___ take subway or trolley.

and I...

LAND POLLUTION:

My family and I can

    ___ pick up litter around home, streets and city

    ___ remove garbage to more sanitary/safe places.

    ___ plant trees.

    ___ use living Christmas trees. and.................

WATER POLLUTION: My family and I

    ___ don't put cleaning chemicals in the ground.

    ___ don't put dirty oil in the ground, but recycle it.

    ___ pick garbage out of streams, rivers and off ocean beaches and throw it away.

    ___ don't use streams or rivers as a bathroom.

    ___ don't waste water.

We can save water by

I save water by

We can keep our rivers and oceans cleaner by

NOISE POLLUTION: To cut down on the noise in my neighborhood and home I

    ___ keep radio/stereo/CD low.

    ___ use non-motorized transportation.

    ___ respect other's sleep patterns.

    ___ use a reasonable outside voice

and:

THE WORLD THAT IS TO COME

Change is constant. The world's changes will hopefully bring peace and harmony. As I grow I would like my adult world

The world of tomorrow can be different. I can make a difference by sharing the me described on these pages. Some of the changes I would like to see are

My world of tomorrow would have this kind of government:

My world of tomorrow would share and trade with

In my world of tomorrow all the people would

The jobs of tomorrow will be

The building of tomorrow will be

The animals would

The parks and zoos would

The problems of today

My friends and I

Change is a part of growth - physical and mental. As I continue to grow, more and more changes will not only take place in the world, but in me as well. The biggest change I foresee will be

The future is mine. I help determine what tomorrow will bring.

I decide if I am going to be happy or sad. I can make a difference in who I am, what I am, where I am going, and how I am going to get there. Day by day I am in a living and ever growing process of **BECOMING ME**. I am the best me that can be.

My next book will be called,

ANSWERS to *Do You Know?*

Who speaks every language? (an echo)

What did the man get when he stole the calendar? (365 days)

In what month people talk least? (February - the shortest month)

Why the little inkspots cried? (Their mother was in the pen doing a long sentence)

What a spendthrift saves and a miser spends? (nothing)

What makes the Tower of Pisa lean? (it never eats)

What is broken every time you say its name? (silence)

Why couldn't Eve get the measles? (because she'd Adam)